December 2015

To my dear
friend Juliet.

I thought you
could use this
book any it's
insigate:
how tai ...
I enjoy it.
Hope you do.
♡ Darla

Praise for *The Fringe Hours*

"Turner's transparency about her life, as well as the survey comments from other women in the book, are refreshingly candid and compassionate. Her book extends grace, hope, and inspiration to the reader."

—*Bookpage*

"Commitments, responsibilities, and social expectations make free time seem like selfish use of a precious resource. Even Christian culture can seem to push for busier and busier lives to feel fruitful. Jessica N. Turner gives a welcome perspective: there are enough hours for everything to get done and some to spare for the betterment of oneself without guilt."

—*Life:Beautiful*

"Do you feel overwhelmed with life and everything you're juggling? Do you wish you had time to recharge your batteries, but your to-do list is so long that the idea seems like an impossibility? . . . In *The Fringe Hours*, Jessica unveils her secrets to success and gives you the tools, tips, and techniques you can use to find time in your full schedule to refresh yourself and refill your tank too. This book is a must-read for busy women everywhere!"

—**Crystal Paine**, founder of MoneySavingMom.com
and *New York Times* bestselling author
of *Say Goodbye to Survival Mode*

"I want to give *The Fringe Hours* to every woman in my life, because this is the conversation we're having over and over, at soccer practice and church and crammed between meetings. Jessica's practical style made me feel like another way is possible. I love this book!"

—**Shauna Niequist**, author of *Bread & Wine*

"Jessica Turner has done an enormous favor to women who are exhausted from struggling to fit it all in, feeling pressure to be perfect and guilty if they don't put themselves last. *The Fringe Hours* is like one gigantic permission slip to carve out some space in your day for the things that give you joy and feed your soul. . . . Making the most of the margins of time is the first step toward, as Turner writes, crafting a good life."

—**Brigid Schulte**, author of the *New York Times* bestselling *Overwhelmed:
Work, Love, and Play When No One Has the Time*

"Jessica is a fantastic teacher—through her own life, she models for those of us in the thick of life that we're never too busy to be a good friend, to work hard, and to invest our whole heart into our God-given passions. I'm so thankful that she selflessly shares her wisdom for the rest of us—my life is richer and braver because of her."

—**Tsh Oxenreider**, author of *Notes from a Blue Bike: The Art of Living Intentionally in a Chaotic World*

"We live in a culture where far too often, women's creative passions get squashed and squeezed right out of their lives. Jessica Turner's *The Fringe Hours* is an honest and encouraging account of how women can make time for what fills them up most. I hope it inspires many women to once again embrace their passions."

—**Tara Sophia Mohr**, author of *Playing Big*

"Whether you are yearning to pursue the passions of your heart, take better care of yourself, or invest time and energy into what really matters, *The Fringe Hours* holds the key. . . . This book does not offer a one-size-fits-all solution but rather a deep look inward to help you live in a more fulfilling and meaningful way."

—**Rachel Macy Stafford**, *New York Times* bestselling author of *Hands Free Mama*

"*The Fringe Hours* offers inspiration to become more mindful about your daily life—to identify the snippets of time you'd normally find frustrating or boring and flip them into windows of opportunity to fuel your interests and passions. . . . I'm inspired to seek out fringe minutes during the day and spend them well."

—**Christine Koh**, coauthor, *Minimalist Parenting: Enjoy Modern Family Life More by Doing Less*

"Have you ever claimed to be busy but lost an hour to Pinterest? In this gentle yet no-nonsense book, Jessica nudges us to question how we spend our time and to find ways to bring joy into the little and large spaces of our lives."

—**Laura Vanderkam**, author *168 Hours*

"With each page of *The Fringe Hours*, Jessica offers gentle encouragement, creative ideas, and maintainable solutions that can help us reclaim our time and make our own self-care a top priority."

—**Tracey Clark**, author of *Elevate the Everyday: A Photographic Guide to Picturing Motherhood*

My
FRINGE
HOURS

DISCOVERING *a* MORE CREATIVE
and FULFILLED LIFE

JESSICA N. TURNER

Revell

a division of Baker Publishing Group
Grand Rapids, Michigan

To Elias, Adeline, and Ezra
May you always pursue your passions.
I love you.

© 2015 by Jessica N. Turner

Published by Revell
a division of Baker Publishing Group
P.O. Box 6287, Grand Rapids, MI 49516-6287
www.revellbooks.com

Printed in the United States of America

Library of Congress Cataloging-in-Publication Data
Turner, Jessica N.
    My fringe hours : discovering a more creative and fulfilled life / Jessica N.
Turner.
        pages cm
    ISBN 978-0-8007-2355-2 (cloth)
    1. Christian women—Religious life. I. Title.
BV4527.T874 2015
248.8′43—dc23   2015023282

Some portions of this book have been adapted from *The Fringe Hours: Making Time for You* (Revell, 2015).

Causes of guilt discussed on page 40 are taken from Iyanla Vanzant, "The 3 Reasons People Feel Guilty," Oprah's Lifeclass video, Oprah Winfrey Network, July 30, 2012, https://www.youtube.com/watch?v=GqYyU1tkTVk.

Research described on page 91 can be found at Dr. Jeremy Dean, "Ask for Help: Why People Are Twice as Likely to Assist as You Think," PsyBlog, July 10, 2008, http://www.spring.org.uk/2008/07/ask-for-help-people-twice-as-likely-to.php.

Published in association with literary agent Jenni L. Burke of D.C. Jacobson & Associates, an Author Management Company, www.dcjacobson.com.

15   16   17   18   19   20   21   7   6   5   4   3   2   1

Contents

A Note from Jessica

I don't know you. But I know women like you.

Women who are incredible—incredible co-workers, wives, mothers, friends, volunteers. Yet with each of these roles comes much busyness and often a lack of self-care. Does that sound familiar?

Chances are, you could be doing better job at prioritizing yourself. That's right—you. Whether you know this or not, you should be one of *your own* priorities.

In this book, we are going to take a deep dive into the various elements of your life—from your feelings of guilt to your temptations to play the comparison game, from your many talents and passions to finding the time in your busy schedule to actually pursue those talents and passions.

And yes, no matter how busy and packed you think your life is, time for you *does* exist.

Now, please understand, this is not a time-management book because *My Fringe Hours* is not about doing more. It's about discovering ways to help you *be* more creative and *live* more fulfilled.

How you go about this discovery process is up to you. This book is built on nine principles for finding and embracing the need for self-care. Start at the beginning and work through it in five to ten minutes a day. Or skip around, answering questions as they strike your fancy.

Whatever your approach, I hope that by the end, your eyes will be opened to the importance of practicing self-care, what passions of yours have been waiting to be unleashed, and where to find the time to actually begin pursuing them. Ultimately, finding your fringe hours is about becoming a healthier, happier, more complete you.

Warmly,

Jessica

If you are hungry for more on this topic, including stories from dozens of women from around the country, read *The Fringe Hours: Making Time for You.*

"It is our privilege
and
our adventure
to discover our own
special light."

EVELYN DUNBAR

What's Your Normal?

*F*irst things first. Let's get a baseline of what life looks like for you right now. What is "normal" for you? Answer the following short survey to capture a snapshot of your everyday life. Home, work, hobbies, struggles—it's all covered in these twenty questions.

These questions are the same ones I asked women when I started writing *The Fringe Hours: Making Time for You.* More than two thousand women responded to them on an online survey. You can see how your answers compare to other women's responses by checking out the survey results in the back of the book.

But remember, the most common responses might not be *your* responses. And that's okay. The *My Fringe Hours* journey is a personal one, tailored to you, your life, your story, and your hopes and dreams. In the pages ahead, you'll get to explore and experiment, taking you on a path toward a beautiful and fulfilling life.

1. **How much time do you spend weekly on yourself and the things you are passionate about? (Think about hobbies, personal health, etc.)**
   a. Less than an hour
   b. 1–3 hours
   c. 3–5 hours
   d. 5–9 hours
   e. 10–14 hours
   f. 15 hours or more

2. **What kinds of activities do you love to do? (Circle all that apply.)**
   a. Outdoor activities
   b. Exercising
   c. Sewing/knitting/crocheting
   d. Playing an instrument
   e. Crafting
   f. Spa time (getting a massage, facials, etc.)
   g. Reading
   h. Collecting
   i. Scrapbooking
   j. Photography
   k. Cooking/baking
   l. Writing
   m. Blogging
   n. Other: ....

3. **Do you ever do these activities with other people? (Circle all that apply.)**
   a. Yes, with one other person
   b. Yes, with a small group of people
   c. Yes, with a large group of people
   d. No

4. **On a scale from 0 to 10, how satisfied are you with the amount of time you have for yourself?**
   ....

5. **If you had more time, what activities would you do or do more of? (List a few from the options in question 2.)**
   ....
   ....
   ....

6. **During the week, what time do you wake up?**
   a. Before 5:00 a.m.
   b. 5:00 to 5:59 a.m.
   c. 6:00 to 6:59 a.m.
   d. 7:00 to 7:59 a.m.
   e. 8:00 a.m. or later

7. **If you have children, do you wake up before, at the same time as, or after your children?**
   a. Before my children
   b. At the same time as my children
   c. After my children

8. **On average, how many nights a week are you not at home due to other commitments (children's activities, community group, book club, work, etc.)?**

   1   2   3   4   5   6   7

9. **What time do you go to bed?**
   a. Before 9:00 p.m.
   b. 9:00 to 9:59 p.m.
   c. 10:00 to 10:59 p.m.
   d. 11:00 to 11:59 p.m.
   e. 12:00 a.m. or later

10. **If you have children, do you go to bed before, at the same time as, or after your children?**
   a. Before my children
   b. At the same time as my children
   c. After my children

11. **When do you find time to do the things that you love? (Circle all that apply.)**
   a. In the morning
   b. At lunch time
   c. In the afternoon
   d. At dinnertime
   e. In the evening
   f. During other activities (e.g., kids' practices, waiting in line, etc.)

12. **What are the barriers to making time for yourself? (Circle all that apply.)**
   a. Work
   b. Kids
   c. Household responsibilities
   d. Spouse/significant other
   e. Finances
   f. Church
   g. Group activities
   h. Other: ....

13. **Does someone in your life encourage you to make time for yourself? If so, who? (Circle all that apply.)**
   a. Spouse/significant other
   b. Relative
   c. Friend

14. **Do you have the following devices/ technology in your home? (Circle all that apply.)**
   a. Smartphone
   b. iPad/tablet
   c. E-reader
   d. Cable or satellite TV
   e. Laptop or desktop computer
   f. Internet

15. **Do you pay for any of the following services? (Circle all that apply.)**
   a. Child care
   b. Cleaning service
   c. Lawn service
   d. Laundry service
   e. Meal preparation
   f. Handyman service

16. **Do you keep a calendar? If yes, what type of calendar do you use? (Circle all that apply.)**
   a. Wall calendar
   b. Portable paper planner
   c. Calendar on phone
   d. Calendar on computer (e.g., Google Calendar, Outlook)

17. Do you use any productivity apps (e.g., Evernote, Pocket, Clear, ToDoodle)? If yes, what do you use? How does it help?

....

....

....

....

18. If you make time for yourself, why do you value doing that?

....

....

....

....

19. If you don't make time for yourself, why don't you?

....

....

....

....

20. What do you think is most challenging about being a woman today?

....

....

....

....

The great thing about those survey questions is that they don't have "right answers." The most important thing is that you write down your truth. With that in mind, let's do a gut check.

As you completed the survey, did anything you wrote down, thought about, or felt stand out to you?

....

....

....

Did any of the questions make you feel uncomfortable or frustrated? If so, which ones and why?

....

....

....

How did it feel to acknowledge something that you love to do?

....

....

....

Did you feel satisfied thinking about time spent on that passion, or did you wish you could do it more often?

....

....

....

LORE

opefully the survey helped you scratch the surface of what your life looks like right now. In this section we are going to dive a bit deeper into your heart and the struggles you face when it comes to making time for you. Because trust me, your struggle to make *you* a priority is real, and you are not alone.

One of the biggest reasons women avoid taking care of themselves is because they wrestle with balance and priorities. They find it challenging to juggle work, life, and family, and oftentimes they make the decision to put themselves last. Another common struggle women deal with is feelings of self-imposed pressure and guilt. Frequently women are their own toughest critics, battling a barrage of unrealistic expectations they never quite manage to fulfill.

These matters of the heart and mind need to be explored and addressed before you can truly start caring for yourself. Let's first take some time to recognize and overcome the internal obstacles that can hinder your journey toward a more fulfilling life.

Fringe Principle 1

||||||||||

I believe in cultivating balance in my commitments and within myself.

*T*he modern woman struggles with balance on a daily basis. It's a pursuit that feels elusive at times, an ideal that only seems to happen to other people. Many of the women cited in the survey that the struggle to achieve balance is the most challenging part of everyday life. Considering the numerous roles that women play, this struggle is no surprise.

While *perfect* balance cannot be attained, it can be used as a guiding principle for life choices. More importantly, doing so will push you to become intentional about making yourself a priority.

Balance can be defined as a satisfying arrangement of elements and emotional stability. Using this definition of balance is an excellent guide for finding the freedom to say no and the fortitude to create healthy boundaries. Ultimately, balance will lead you toward a more gratifying, life-giving path.

Considering Balance

What does balance look like for you? Do you have commitments in your life that are good things but maybe aren't good for this season of your life?

In the center of the scale on the next page, describe your current season of life. What or who are your top five priorities right now?

At the high end of the scale, write down some of the things you wish you had more time for.

At the low end of the scale, write down the various commitments you have or activities you're involved in right now. These are the items currently weighing down your schedule. By reducing or eliminating them, you can make your scale more balanced. Consider whether anything should be eliminated from your schedule so that you'll have more time for the things you long to do.

Just because something is a *good thing* doesn't mean it is good for this *moment* in your life.

"Most of us
have trouble juggling.
The woman who
says she doesn't is
someone whom I admire
but have never met."

BARBARA WALTERS

Cultivating Balance in Your Commitments

While consistent balance may be difficult to achieve, these tips may help you find more space in your days.

1. **Learn to say no.** For any kind of balance to exist, you must embrace the word *no*. Don't be afraid to use it. Remember, saying no is not a bad thing. You shouldn't feel guilty about saying no—even when you turn down a good thing—when it means you are saying yes to something better. And sometimes taking care of yourself is the better thing.

2. **Learn from your mistakes.** Sometimes you're going to overbook yourself and life is going to be too full. Learn from those seasons. Once you come out on the other side, ask yourself what you could have done differently. For instance, could you have said no to something or scheduled an activity for another month?

3. **Evaluate what matters.** Continuously review your schedule and make sure everything is necessary. A quote I have on my desk reads, "If what you do doesn't matter to you, it's really not going to matter to anyone else." Work to fill your life with the things that matter most to you.

4. **Reduce distractions.** Sometimes balance can be achieved just by turning off your phone, computer, or other technological devices. Or you might need to find a quiet place in your home or out in nature to be less distracted.

Yes or No?

Women receive countless requests for their time. Appeals to help the PTA. A boss's request for working overtime. A friend's invitation to go shopping. Sometimes we *can't* say no. But most of the time, we get to make a choice. Remember, too much of a good thing is still too much. So choose wisely. And leave time for the things that matter most.

Think of five things you've recently been asked to do. Are they things you *need* to do? Or are they things that would be nice to do but not things you *have* to say yes to? (A friend once told me, "If it isn't a heck yes, it's a no," which is a good rule of thumb.) Record those five requests on the next page along with how you will respond or have already responded.

Request	Need to do?	Nice to do?	How to respond
1.			
2.			
3.			
4.			
5.			

Do you have enough time to do everything in the grid?

Yes

No

If not, what "good things" will you say no to in order to have time for what's best?

....

....

....

Cultivating Balance within Yourself

Balance is about more than just the activities you *do*. The following actions can help you create better balance within yourself as well. Which ones resonate with you the most?

1. Extend yourself grace. Balance is rarely simple, as our lives and responsibilities often change. Don't be hard on yourself on the challenging days.

2. Take care of your health. Oftentimes when we run ourselves ragged, our health suffers. To live a balanced life, you must take care of your body. Eat well, go to the doctor for checkups, exercise, and get enough sleep.

3. Give and receive love. We were created for relationships. Love well each day.

4. Pray. Make time each day to pray and be with the Lord. God is your comfort and rock. You do not have to go through a single day without him.

5. Express gratitude. Take time each day to write down what you are thankful for. Research shows that people who keep a gratitude list are happier people.

Stress Alert

We all have the occasional stressed-out day. But are high stress levels your everyday norm? Consider your top five stressors, as they may indicate that something has gotten out of balance in your life.

List your top five stressors:

1. ....
2. ....
3. ....
4. ....
5. ....

Are any of these stressors caused by commitments you could say no to the next time around? If so, cross them off your list. Consider what life would look like without them. Write down two words to describe how it would make you feel to eliminate these items:

....

Some stressors are unavoidable. We all go through seasons where stressful people or life circumstances are beyond our control. If you can't eliminate these stressors from your life, write what you can do to minimize their impact.

....
....
....
....
....

I Will Live a Life That Cultivates Balance

What do you need to do to cultivate balance in your commitments and within yourself?

....

....

....

....

....

What one step will you take this week to eliminate something that causes you to feel stressed and out of balance?

....

....

....

....

....

Finish this sentence: *Cultivating balance will help me have a more creative and fulfilled life by . . .*

....

....

....

....

....

Fringe Principle 2

||||||||||||||

I believe in letting go of self-imposed pressures.

Sometimes women can become our own worst enemies when it comes to making time for ourselves. A lifestyle of pleasing everyone to the point of emptiness is a reality for many. And it happens when we take the desire for balance and couple it with the unreasonable expectation that we need to be everything for everyone. While deep down women recognize that this lofty goal is unachievable, the self-imposed pressure still leaves many drained, physically and emotionally.

Do you believe (maybe almost subconsciously) that being everything to everyone is what's required of you?

This is a lie.

In fact, living as though you have to be everything for everyone will suck the life right out of you. The flame of your personal passions that once burned bright in your soul slowly fades to embers, barely glowing.

The sooner you stop this ugly cycle of trying to do it all and be everything, the sooner you'll experience freedom.

Freedom in your schedule.

Freedom from the "I should do this" voice in your head.

Freedom to reignite your passions and pursue what you love.

You don't have to be bound by unreasonable expectations of what you "should do" anymore. And you don't have to appease an imaginary Pinterest-perfect persona that doesn't exist. Let those self-imposed pressures go. You'll find that it's more than enough to be just who you were created to be.

Too Much Pressure

Do you put pressure on yourself when it comes to your parenting? Your home? Your marriage? Your work? In the circles below, list the pressures you put on yourself.

After filling in these circles, put an X through each item as a tangible way of releasing these pressures from your life.

Today's women are bombarded with unrealistic images of what it means to be the perfect woman, the perfect wife, and the perfect mom. But a woman's self-worth isn't based on idealized perfection. We must stop pursuing these unrealistic images and instead embrace a healthy balance that recognizes our limitations. Nobody can be perfect. But anybody can seek joy despite their imperfections.

Many of the things we think matter actually don't. Does it really hurt to leave the dinner dishes until morning? Will a little dust truly harm your family? If not, maybe you need to consider letting go of these little imperfections. What *does* matter is loving others and loving ourselves.

In your *glorious imperfection*, you can still shine *beautifully bright*.

In these boxes, write words representing what you strive to be or any unrealistic things you strive to attain:

In these boxes, write what makes you uniquely you and why others love you:

"Until you make peace with who you are, you'll never be content with what you have."

DORIS MORTMAN

Ways of Overcoming Self-Imposed Pressures

1. **Let it go.** This might be easier said than done, but when a pressure weighs down on you, acknowledge it, but then let it go. Do not let it hold you hostage.

2. **Worry less.** Oftentimes a self-imposed pressure will be compounded by feelings of worry and what-ifs. Instead of worrying, let your voice of reason speak into your life.

3. **Compare less.** Keep your eyes and thoughts on your story, and don't compare your situation to someone else's. Comparison breeds resentment, not healthy living.

4. **Eliminate negative self-talk.** Don't let your mind think or mouth speak things that are negative about you, your actions, and your worth.

5. **Manage expectations.** Be reasonable and don't set the bar so high that you set yourself up for failure. Ultimately having reasonable expectations will keep the pressure from becoming too great.

Which of the ideas above seems like the one you most need to focus on? Circle the tactic you will try to use next time you feel those self-imposed pressures mounting.

I Will Live a Life That Is Free of Self-Imposed Pressures

What unrealistic expectations have I been trying to live up to?

....

....

....

....

How have these pressures I've been placing on myself impacted my time for self-care?

....

....

....

....

What do I need to do to stop letting the buck stop with me?

....

....

....

....

Finish this sentence: *Eliminating self-imposed pressures will help me have a more creative and fulfilled life by . . .*

....

....

....

....

Fringe Principle 3

||||||||||||||

I believe that guilt and comparison do not belong in my life.

*G*uilt and comparison are two additional obstacles that prevent women from living fulfilled lives. In the survey, many women cited guilt as a reason they didn't take care of themselves. They said things like:

I am overcommitted and can always find a reason to guilt myself into not doing things for myself or making time for myself. —Andrea

Guilt . . . I usually feel like I should be doing something else other than making time for myself. I feel like I'm not making the best use of my time when the purpose is me. —Lisa

And regarding comparison, women also struggled:

It's hard not to look at my peers and think, "Gosh, they really have it all together." —Samantha

We see others who seem to be doing it all and have it all with what looks like little effort, so we think that is what our lives should look like as well. —Katherine

Feelings of guilt and comparison are unhealthy, yet so often women let these traps dictate their actions and emotions. In this section, take some time to unpack your own feelings, learn how to better respond, and ultimately find freedom.

"Nobody
can make you
feel inferior
without
your consent."

ELEANOR ROOSEVELT

Causes of Guilt

Popular author and speaker Iyanla Vanzant said that guilt has three main causes:

1. We know that what we are doing is out of order, but we do it anyway.
2. We know we cause hurt, harm, or danger to someone.
3. We disappoint or upset someone we love or care about.

The cause we're discussing here is a combination of #1 and #3. For some women it feels "out of order" to read a book or go for a walk when chores still need to be done. Other women worry about disappointing a spouse, child, co-worker, friend, or someone else if they choose to do something for themselves instead of for the other person.

Which cause most often creates guilt in you? Why?

....

....

....

....

....

....

On a scale of 1 to 10, how often do you feel guilty in a typical day?

1	2	3	4	5	6	7	8	9	10
Rarely				A few times					All the time

What do you do when you feel guilty? Does that emotion impact the choices you make, and if so, how?

....

....

....

....

....

....

Permission to Not Feel Guilty

Here are some ways to give yourself permission to make time for yourself and not feel guilty about it:

1. **Tell your husband or a friend,** "I need to take better care of myself. Will you help me make 'me time' each week?"

2. **Post a note** somewhere visible reminding you, "I am worth it. I matter. I am valuable."

3. **Leave a chore for later** and go read a book, sew, or just be still for twenty minutes. The chore will still be there.

4. **Pray** that God would help you remove this self-inflicted guilt from your life.

5. **Practice self-care with a friend.** The accountability may be just the push you need to live a life that includes time for yourself.

6. **Breathe.** It's going to be okay.

Which one of these ideas would help you feel less guilty and why?

....

....

....

....

....

....

From Judgment to Celebration

We need to prevent ourselves from judging other women. So what should we do instead? If a judgmental thought comes into your head, try these ideas:

1. **Turn the negative into something positive.** Instead of judging the woman who brings store-bought food to the potluck, commend her for not spending excessive time in the kitchen.
2. **Consider the roots.** Are you judging that person because you are envious? Dissatisfied? What is the emotion tied to that reaction? Deal with the root cause of your judgment.
3. **Talk to her.** Many times we judge because we don't know a person's story. Get to know her and her story. You might be surprised at what you learn.
4. **Embrace acceptance.** We are all uniquely made. Accept a woman just as she is and celebrate what makes her unique.

"Turn moments of *comparison* into *catalysts* for *celebration*."

THE FRINGE HOURS

Be You

Have you ever looked at other women in your life and wondered, "How do they do it?" Did you follow up that question with, "Why can't I seem to pull it off like they do?"

When we start comparing ourselves to others, we can quickly feel overwhelmed. That's because no one can live up to the strengths of every woman combined. You are unique. Embrace your own abilities, and learn to enjoy the strengths of others without pressuring yourself to make them your own. Celebrating others is so much better than comparing yourself to them.

I'm different because ...

I'm different because ...

Who do you tend to compare yourself to? Write their names under the figures.

For each person you listed, write down one way that your personality, strengths, or life circumstances are *different* from theirs.

Next time you find yourself wanting to be like someone else, take a breath and let that feeling go. You don't have to compare yourself to any of these women, because you're uniquely you!

....

I'm different because...

....

....

....

....

....

I'm different because...

....

....

....

....

Ways to Avoid the Comparison Trap

You were created to be a passionate, vibrant woman. Feelings of guilt and comparison will do nothing but steal life's joy away from you. When you feel comparison creeping into your mind, prevent those thoughts by doing the following:

1. **Practice gratitude.** When you sense yourself comparing, turn that comparison on its head with a message of gratitude.

2. **Minimize social media.** This might mean going on social media sites less often or unfollowing people who cause you to stumble.

3. **Say no to situations that will breed resentment.** If attending an event or saying yes to a project is only going to cause you to judge or be ungrateful, then don't do it. It's not worth it.

4. **Celebrate what makes you special.** No one else is just like you. Celebrate your unique gifts, accomplishments, and work done well.

5. **Compliment others.** By complimenting people, you are focusing on what makes them special, which will impact your perspective about them.

I Will Live a Life That Is Free of Guilt and Comparison

How have guilt and/or comparison kept me from living a satisfying life?

....

....

....

....

What truths do I need to embrace in order to be free of guilt?

....

....

....

....

How can I celebrate my unique gifts when I try to compare myself to other women?

....

....

....

....

Finish this sentence: *Ridding myself of the damaging feelings of guilt and comparison will help me have a more creative and fulfilled life by . . .*

....

....

....

....

DISC

OVER

*H*ave you identified those obstacles that prevent you from living a life that includes time for you? It isn't going to be an overnight change, but acknowledging where you can improve is a huge first step. Unbalanced lives, unrealistic expectations, and guilt and comparison can all prevent you from practicing self-care. Moving toward freedom in those areas is critical to making the most of your fringe hours.

Now that you've explored and overcome some of the hurdles to taking time for your passions, you're ready to focus on discovery. Where can you find those fringe hours in your days? How do you want to spend those precious "you" hours? What passions do you want to pursue? This section will help you answer those questions and start making self-care a regular part of your days.

Using your fringe hours well will help you live a more creative and fulfilled life—and that's the heart of this book. So read, reflect, and enjoy unpacking the secrets that will inspire you to find that time.

Fringe Principle 4

||||||||||||

I believe that I can make time for myself.

his is a big principle—the key to this entire book. So much of what you're exploring in these pages will hinge on time and using it well.

Busyness is often blamed as the reason women neglect their own self-care. Too many other things need their attention. But if you truly desire a well-rounded, healthy, and happy life, you must make time for yourself in the middle of it all.

Even on the busiest days, you can find fringe hours to experience pleasure, creativity, and fulfillment. You just need to identify and leverage those pockets of time that often go underused or wasted altogether. This is not about doing more—it's about living better.

Your fringe hours may not seem like much at first. Five minutes here, half an hour there—those little chunks of time can easily slip by. However, when fringe hours are recognized for their collective potential and used for pursuing passions, life change can happen.

From writing a card to journaling or reading a book, fringe hours can yield a great deal of fruit. The aspiration you thought was just a dream begins to take shape. Little by little, happiness abounds and your relationships prosper. Turn the page, and let's discover your fringe hours.

"We can't practice compassion with other people if we don't treat ourselves kindly."

BRENÉ BROWN

Defining Fringe Hours

What is a "fringe hour"? Let's dive into the words' definitions.

Fringe:

1. a decorative border of thread, cord, or the like, usually hanging loosely from a raveled edge or separate strip
2. an outer edge; margin; periphery

Hour:

1. 1/24th of a day; 60 minutes
2. a short or limited period of time
3. a particular or appointed time

When you put these definitions together, you get a fringe hour: a limited or appointed piece of time that is found in the margins of a day. But that's not all. Fringe is something decorative. Think about it: fringe typically makes a piece of clothing, an accessory, or an object more beautiful. And fringe does the same for life. Activities and passions pursued during the fringe hours make your life more beautiful. They make you feel more alive and more uniquely you.

"*Great things* are not done by impulse, but by a series of *small things* brought together."

VINCENT VAN GOGH

Time Tracking

If you don't know where fringe hours can be found in your days, try tracking your time for a week. After completing this exercise, you will be able to better understand where your time goes, what changes you might need to make in your schedule, and where fringe hours can be maximized.

Use the charts on the following pages to track your time for the next week. Write down everything from the car pool line to household chores. The more details the better. You might be surprised by what you discover.

"Don't say you don't have *enough time*. You have exactly the *same number* of hours per day that were given to Helen Keller, Louis Pasteur, Michelangelo, Mother Teresa, Leonardo da Vinci, Thomas Jefferson and Albert Einstein."

H. JACKSON BROWN JR.

Time Tracking: Days 1–4

Time	Day 1	Day 2	Day 3	Day 4
5:30				
6:00				
6:30				
7:00				
7:30				
8:00				
8:30				
9:00				
9:30				
10:00				
10:30				
11:00				
11:30				
12:00				
12:30				
1:00				
1:30				
2:00				
2:30				

Time Tracking: Days 1–4 (Continued)

Time	Day 1	Day 2	Day 3	Day 4
3:00				
3:30				
4:00				
4:30				
5:00				
5:30				
6:00				
6:30				
7:00				
7:30				
8:00				
8:30				
9:00				
9:30				
10:00				
10:30				
11:00				
11:30				
12:00				

Time Tracking: Days 5–7

Time	Day 5	Day 6	Day 7
5:30			
6:00			
6:30			
7:00			
7:30			
8:00			
8:30			
9:00			
9:30			
10:00			
10:30			
11:00			
11:30			
12:00			
12:30			
1:00			
1:30			
2:00			
2:30			

Time Tracking: Days 5–7 (Continued)

Time	Day 5	Day 6	Day 7
3:00			
3:30			
4:00			
4:30			
5:00			
5:30			
6:00			
6:30			
7:00			
7:30			
8:00			
8:30			
9:00			
9:30			
10:00			
10:30			
11:00			
11:30			
12:00			

Now that you've tracked your time, reflect on the process. Really review at your week and ask yourself these questions:

What items are nonnegotiables in your schedule (for example, work, taking kids to school, etc.)?

....

....

....

....

What time was wasted?

....

....

....

What activities could be streamlined in your schedule? (For instance, does doing laundry every day make sense, or would it be better to do it as a marathon on one day?)

....

....

....

....

Are you doing too much? If so, what can you eliminate or get help doing?

....

....

....

Did you do anything just because it would have made you feel guilty to not do it? If so, what?

....

....

....

....

Would it be helpful to ask for or hire help for any of the things you spent time on during the week? If so, what do you need help with and is getting help feasible?

....

....

....

....

Did you take time for yourself? If so, how much time?

....

....

....

....

Overall, how did you feel this week? Happy? Tired? Stressed? How did these emotions impact you and your activities?

....

....

....

....

....

....

....

....

....

Finding Your Fringe Hours

Here are some common times of day when you may have fringe hours available:

 Mornings—If your mornings are frantic, you're starting your day at an unhealthy place. But if you wake up early and start the day with time for you, you are better equipped to handle whatever comes your way.

 Lunch time—Taking some time for yourself at lunch can help you return to your work with rejuvenated energy. A big to-do list might tempt you to forgo the break, but when you take the time, you usually accomplish more in the long run.

 Breaks/times of waiting—On average, people wait forty-five to sixty minutes a day. Consider what times of waiting you experience during a day and how you might use that time better. Those little pockets of time can add up to a lot of creativity and joy if you fill them with things you love.

 Nights—Evenings often offer extended time to refuel and enjoy personal time. If possible, limit your nights out during the week, and you can reclaim some of that time for yourself. Evenings spent investing in yourself often translate to more energy the next day to invest in others.

 Weekends—Many women watch the weekend hours dwindle away as they try to tackle everything they didn't get done during the rest of the week. Don't fall into that trap. Plan your weekends the same way you plan your week, with time for yourself among your priorities.

Could you have fringe hours during any of these times? Rank these times in order of likelihood that you would use that period of time for yourself.

.... Mornings

.... Lunch time

.... Breaks/times of waiting

.... Nights

.... Weekends

If you had one hour to do anything you wanted right now, what would you do? Where would you go?

....

....

....

....

What is it about this thing that makes you happy?

....

....

....

....

What's in Your Pockets?

We all have them: those little pockets of time throughout our day when we're "in between." A fifteen-minute window between the morning car pool and Bible study at church. The half hour you spend sitting on the sidelines during soccer practice.

All too often, we fill these moments with mindless activities such as flipping through phone apps, watching a TV talk show, scrolling the latest social media updates. But with a little planning, you can make these precious pockets of time into some of your most enjoyable moments of the day.

"You will never *find time* for anything. If you want time, you must *make it*."

CHARLES BIXTON

What do you typically do during those five- to thirty-minute windows of "free" moments you find in your days? List a few habits below.

....

....

....

....

....

....

Consider your list carefully. Do those activities make you feel creative? Fill you with inspiration? Allow you to enjoy something you love? Do those moments make you feel more *you*? Or are you just mindlessly passing time?

....

....

....

....

....

....

I Will Live a Life That Makes Time for Me

The best times I have discovered for harnessing fringe hours in my day:

....

....

....

....

Time-wasters I want to avoid:

....

....

....

....

One specific fringe hour (or a collection of moments that equal one hour) that I will give to myself this week:

....

....

....

....

Finish this sentence: *Making time for me will help me have a more creative and fulfilled life by . . .*

....

....

....

....

....

Fringe Principle 5

||||||||||||

I believe that pursuing my passions is life-giving and life changing.

We're all uniquely made with passions and interests. For some, a run on a quiet trail invigorates them. For others, it's creating a beautiful dress from a few yards of fabric. Whatever that thing is, we all have a passion inside of us.

All too often, though, women push aside the desire to pursue these passions. Instead of cultivating our interests, we say, "Someday." And that someday is pushed aside for days, weeks, months, even years. Does this sound familiar to you?

Living a life with no room for your passionate pursuits prevents you from fully living out the life God has for you. So as you explore what this principle means for your life, it's important to embrace it at its core. This is not a principle to be lukewarm about. Experience the life-giving, life-changing impact of passionate living by saying *YES*.

Yes, I want this.

Yes, I need this.

Yes, I am worth it.

YES.

When you live a life that includes the pursuit of your passions, you will be your best self. You'll shine brighter, love bigger, and be happier.

When was the last time you enjoyed doing something so much that you completely lost track of the time? What were you doing?

....

....

....

....

....

....

....

What activities do you look forward to every time they get scheduled on the calendar?

....

....

....

....

....

....

"It is best to *learn as we go*,
not *go as we have learned*."

LESLIE JEANNE SAHLER

What makes your heart race? What gets you excited?

....

....

....

....

....

....

....

Is there a hobby you would like to pursue but never have? If so, what is it and what has prevented you from doing it?

....

....

....

....

....

....

....

Identify Your Passions

For many women, it's been so long since they actively pursued their passions that they aren't sure *what* they are passionate about. They're so busy helping everyone else achieve their dreams that when they stop to consider their own, they come up short. If you aren't sure what your passions are, here are a few ways you can (re)discover them.

1. **Look back to your childhood.** What were your favorite things to do as a child? How did those activities make you feel?

   ....
   ....
   ....
   ....
   ....

2. **Think about who inspires you.** People who are inspiring to us often evoke emotions in us that aren't right on the surface. We just need to pay attention to the people who pull out these feelings in us. Who inspires you and why?

   ....
   ....
   ....
   ....
   ....

3. **Make a list:** Put a line through every item that you do not enjoy and a circle around each activity that you do enjoy when you have the time.

Biking	Scrapbooking
Exercising	Photography
Yoga	Cooking/baking
Painting	Writing
DIY projects	Blogging
Sports	Graphic design
Gardening	Genealogy
Drawing	Hunting
Sewing/needlework	Fishing
Knitting/crocheting	Horseback riding
Playing an instrument	Videography
Crafting	Building
Spa time (massage, facial, etc.)	Volunteering
	Traveling
Reading	Other: ....
Collecting	

4. **Create an inspiration board.** Put together a board of things that inspire you: books, color swatches, photos, quotes, and so on. As you look over your collection, a sense of who you are and what you love will emerge.

Roadblocks

As you consider your life right now, are you making time to pursue your interests? Or do your passions sit on a shelf while everything else eats away your time and energy? On a scale of 1 to 10, how often do you make your passions a priority?

1	2	3	4	5	6	7	8	9	10
Always									Never

Sometimes roadblocks appear on the path of pursuing your passions, even when you have the best intentions of making time for yourself. Life is challenging and obstacles will come up.

"You can't wait for *inspiration*. You have to *go after it* with a club."

JACK LONDON

What are the biggest roadblocks preventing you from making time for your passions? Circle all that apply.

The good news is that roadblocks don't have to keep you from moving forward. They just might require you to break out of your routine and take a different route. Pick one item that you circled and brainstorm several ideas for how you might minimize or hand off responsibilities in that area in order to make time for yourself.

....

....

....

....

....

....

"You are never
too busy
to make time for
what you love."

JESSICA N. TURNER

Preventing Interruptions

Interruptions can wreak havoc on the time we commit to ourselves. They might come from your spouse, your children, your roommate, or your phone—but whatever they are, they can easily eat away at the fringe hours in your day. Here are four ways to minimize those interruptions:

1. **Let people know you are not available.** Be straight-forward. When you need some time for yourself, tell your family that you cannot be interrupted. Ask them to respect your time.

2. **Close the door.** This might seem obvious, but a closed door is an easy signal that says "Do not disturb." You may even want to add a sign to the door as a reminder.

3. **Leave the house.** Sometimes you just have to leave the house to ensure that you won't be interrupted. Is there some-where else you could go to enjoy the activity you've chosen?

4. **Silence your cell phone.** Don't let those incoming texts and emails distract you. They can wait until later. If you are taking time just for you, silence your phone.

Who or what tends to interrupt you the most while you are trying to enjoy time alone? Which of these strategies could help you stop those interruptions?

....

....

....

....

....

I Will Pursue My Passions

As you've considered what you are passionate about, I'm sure you have identified some activities you are itching to do. Now it's time to take action and *do them*! Buy supplies for that project. Sign up for that class. It's time to move.

One passion/activity I want to learn more about or do more often:

....

....

....

....

My "next step" in making this activity happen:

....

....

....

....

Finish this sentence: *Pursuing my passions will help me have a more creative and fulfilled life by . . .*

....

....

....

....

Fringe Principle 6

||||||||||||

I believe that taking care of my mind, body, and soul is important.

*F*ringe hours are about caring for you—investing in the passions and interests that make you unique. But in order to do that, you also need to invest in *yourself*.

Your mind.

Your body.

Your soul.

Only you can be fully attentive to your needs in these areas. And it's important to make time for them. A significant part of living a more creative and fulfilled life includes taking care of yourself physically, emotionally, and spiritually.

But caring for yourself can be difficult. Many women struggle with this because they're stretched thin taking care of others, including spouses, children, and aging parents. But when women neglect themselves, not only do they suffer, but so does everyone else.

So embrace the need for good mental, physical, and spiritual health. Because when you give care to yourself, you will have more to pour into others and be your best self.

Self-Care Checkup

Complete a brief evaluation of your current self-care. How much time are you currently spending taking care of your mind, body, and soul?

Things I do to care for my mind:

....

....

....

....

Things I do to care for my body:

....

....

....

....

Things I do to care for my soul:

....

....

....

....

Only you can take care of *you*.

Strong Minds

Have you ever been so busy caring for others that you ended up feeling emotionally frazzled? Without proper self-care, our minds experience a never-ending roller coaster of emotions. Unexpected challenges easily push us over the edge when we're feeling stressed. And our good intentions quickly fade when we become angry and impatient with the people we love most.

Self-care isn't a privilege. It's a necessity for sound mental and emotional health. Schedule set periods of time in your days and weeks to be reserved for your own needs. It's the only way to ensure consistent investment in yourself.

On the scale below, circle your emotion level on a typical day based on these descriptions:

1 = Emotions swinging out of control, feeling constantly overwhelmed

3 = Some emotional ups and downs throughout the day

5 = Peaceful, calm, able to face unexpected challenges with grace for myself and others

1   2   3   4   5

Put a square around the number that you would *like* to experience as your emotional norm.

Are you happy with your current level of mental/emotional stability? Why or why not?

....
....
....
....
....
....

When was the last time you "blew up" because of overwhelming emotions or stress? Describe the situation and how you felt about it afterward:

....
....
....
....
....
....
....
....

What do you do currently to maintain good mental health?

....

....

....

....

....

....

....

In what ways do you neglect your mental health?

....

....

....

....

....

....

....

What are three things you could do to improve your stress management and mental health?

....

....

....

....

....

....

....

Six Habits for a Healthy Body

Grade yourself (A–F) in each of the following areas. For any area that receives a C or below, jot down notes about what could be improved.

Healthy Habit	Grade
Get regular checkups. Do you schedule annual physicals and six-month dental cleanings?	
Pay attention to your body. Do you notice and take care of yourself when something feels wrong?	
Drink lots of water. Do you drink 8–9 glasses of water per day?	
Exercise. Do you engage in 150 minutes of physical activity each week?	
Eat healthy. Do you have a balanced diet including fruits, vegetables, lean protein, and whole grains?	
Rest. Do you sleep seven to nine hours each night?	

"Faith is to believe
what you do not see;
the reward of
this faith is to see
what you believe."

ST. AUGUSTINE

Feed Your Soul

Nurturing your spirituality is an important part of self-care. We are created by God and are meant to be in relationship with him. Oftentimes when we neglect ourselves, we're also neglecting our spirituality. We might go through the motions, but we don't experience deep growth.

Here are some simple yet intentional ways to nurture your faith:

- Pray
- Attend church
- Gather with other people
- Read the Bible
- Read spiritual books and blogs

Which of these faith-nurturing activities do you regularly practice? Which would you like to do more?

....

....

....

....

....

Are there certain times of the day when you feel most open to spiritual care? If so, how can you better use this time?

....

....

....

....

Are you satisfied with the amount of time you currently spend nurturing your soul? Why or why not?

....

....

....

....

....

Think about the last time you felt an especially strong connection with God.

Where were you?

What were you doing?

What did you learn about God from that experience?

....

....

....

....

....

....

....

....

....

I Will Care for My Mind, Body, and Soul

One goal I want to reach *this month* for each of the following aspects of self-care:

Mental care

....

....

....

Physical care

....

....

....

Spiritual care

....

....

....

Finish this sentence: *Caring for my own well-being will help me have a more creative and fulfilled life by . . .*

....

....

....

....

....

WELL

*Y*ou have so much potential, and practicing self-care is the best way to ensure that you maximize it. In these final chapters, we'll explore secrets to living well. We'll build on the principles laid out earlier in the book and add to them a few ideas that will help you make the most of your fringe hours.

Some might assume that making time for you is all about being alone, but that's not the case. Investing in community and connecting with others while pursuing your passions will help you live a more well-rounded and meaningful life. In fact, sometimes it's necessary to have others come alongside you in order for you to make time for self-care.

We will also discuss the importance of finding rest. And along the way, we'll discover how embracing joy and practicing gratitude can bring a deeper, more satisfying wholeness to every hour of your days.

Fringe Principle 7

||||||||||||

I believe in embracing help.

Women often have a hard time admitting they need help. We juggle countless activities, attempting to live up to unrealistic expectations with our all-too-realistic resources. Pursuing life like this leaves us feeling overwhelmed and isolated.

Research from Columbia University published in the *Journal of Personality and Social Psychology* found that people grossly underestimated how willing others are to help out—by as much as 100 percent.

One hundred percent!

In other words, people really do enjoy helping others. And not only do they enjoy it, they want to do it. We just need to ask. While some fear popping that question because they view it as a sign of weakness, asking for help actually denotes strength. By recognizing our need for help and requesting the service of others, we are not only recognizing our limitations but also crafting a better life by inviting others into our story in practical and tangible ways. That's not weak—it's wise.

We don't need to do everything alone. Embracing help with everyday tasks will allow you to use your time more intentionally. And that puts you on a path toward a richer, more satisfied version of you.

It's Hard to Accept Help

If you're like most people, asking for help is probably an uneasy task. Why? Perhaps you're worried about what people will think—will they judge you for not being able to do everything on your own? Maybe you're afraid of appearing needy. Maybe you struggle to know who or how to ask. Or maybe you love the idea of having help if only you knew how to pay for it. Identifying the fears or obstacles that keep you from seeking help is the first step toward finding it.

How often do you struggle with asking for help?

1	2	3	4	5	6	7	8	9	10
Never									All the time

Circle each word/phrase that prevents you from asking for help.

Pride   Unconvinced that you need help

Knowing who to ask   Resources/finances

Shyness

Do you struggle with asking for help in certain areas of your life more than others? Rank the areas from most difficult to least difficult, with 1 being the hardest area to ask for help.

.... In the home   .... Work tasks

.... Parenting   .... Hobbies

.... Child care   .... Other: ....

For each the top three most challenging areas, jot down a reason you find it difficult to seek help (pride, knowing who to ask, finances, etc.).

1. ....
   ....
   ....
   ....

2. ....
   ....
   ....
   ....

3. ....
   ....
   ....
   ....

"If we are ever to enjoy life, *now* is the time, not *tomorrow* or next *year*. . . . *Today* should always be our *most wonderful day*."

THOMAS DREIER

Acknowledge Your Limitations

Have you ever made a to-do list, knowing full well you were never going to get to even half the items on your list? Have you ever tried to cram three days' worth of errands or activities into a single afternoon? The end result can be pretty ugly. In our pursuit to be superwoman for a day, we can turn into frustrated wrecks, yelling at our kids or snapping at our co-workers.

Part of the process of asking for help is realizing your limitations. Superwoman looks a lot different in real life than she does in the comic books. The beauty of asking for help is that you allow the other person's strength to shine—and that is a powerful gift to offer someone else. Moreover, when you let go of your pride and accept help from another, you'll free up time to pursue your own strengths and discover (or rediscover) ways for them to shine.

When was the last time you felt completely overwhelmed and why?

....

....

....

....

What areas of your life make you feel ill-equipped or overwhelmed?

....

....

....

....

Do you worry about what people will think if you ask for help? If so, write down the negative judgments you fear:

....

....

....

....

....

....

....

For each of the negative statements you wrote above, rewrite it as a positive statement. (For example, if you wrote, "People will think I'm lazy for not cleaning my own house," you could rewrite that as "I'm blessed in many areas. Having someone help me clean allows me to flourish in those other giftings.")

....

....

....

....

....

....

....

"You can't do
everything,
so don't fall
into the trap
of trying."

MARCUS BUCKINGHAM

Areas in Which to Embrace Help

One woman loves to cook, but she finds laundry and cleaning a constant trial. Someone else has a knack for organizing, but she's overwhelmed by home improvement projects. We're all gifted differently!

In what areas of your life *should* you embrace help? Take a look at the list below and circle the areas where you tend to get most overwhelmed.

Cleaning and organizing

Meal preparation

Home maintenance/improvements

Child care

Work

Exercise

Time alone

For each item you circled, jot down the specific tasks you'd like to receive help with (for example, doing laundry, cleaning bathrooms, making lunches, planting flower beds, painting a room).

....

....

....

....

....

....

....

Five Tips for Asking Your Family to Help

1. **Be proactive, not reactive.** Don't wait until you are overwhelmed and impatient. Ask when you're cool and calm and can negotiate a negative response if you receive one.

2. **Ask at the right time.** Ask for help at a time when your family is feeling rested and fully present. If your husband needs a cup of coffee to get going, hold off on the daily "honey-do" requests until he's had a few sips. On the flip side, if your kids are at their brightest in the morning, have them work on some household chores before they run out of steam.

3. **Be mindful of what is going on in your family members' lives.** If they are facing their own deadlines or an especially busy day, be thoughtful. Maybe you need to seek help somewhere else.

4. **Ask in person.** No one likes to come home to a note ordering them to do this or that. Try to plan ahead so you can ask your kids or husband in person.

5. **Say thank you.** Sometimes we forget simple manners with the people we're closest to. But a few simple "thank-yous" can fill your home with a spirit of gratitude.

Help with Hobbies

Finding help isn't limited to your everyday responsibilities. You can also get help with a hobby that you enjoy or want to learn more about. Taking a class or having someone teach you a skill can save you time (and sometimes money). Most importantly, it will also help you improve at something that you can enjoy in your fringe hours.

If you want help with your hobbies, here are some ways to get it:

1. **A friend:** If you have a friend who is particularly talented at a skill, chances are she'd be happy to help you learn.
2. **Community resources:** From churches to libraries and creative programs, organizations in most communities offer classes for learning a variety of skills. Do research online to see what's available near you.
3. **Conferences:** Events dedicated to specific hobbies are a great opportunity to meet like-minded people while learning or improving a skill.
4. **Online:** Numerous websites offer online classes and instructional videos. Teaching for knitting, painting, photography, woodworking, and much more can be found with just a few keystrokes.

What is one new hobby that you would like to try this month? Why does it interest you?

....

....

....

....

Will you need help? If so, how will you get it?

....

....

....

....

....

....

"In this world, we must *help* one another."

JEAN DE LA FONTAINE

Dollars and Sense

Sometimes finances are tight and hiring help may seem like an impossible dream. However, you are worth the investment! It just might take a little creativity to pay for the help you need. Before you give up on getting help, consider giving these ideas a try:

One-Month Trial: How much would it cost for just one month of that child care, cleaning service, or hobby class? Could you give up something for a while in order to give it a try? Maybe you can pack frozen entrees for lunch instead of eating out at work. Or you could sign your child up for one less activity. Or instead of going out to the movies, try family game nights at home. Give it a try, and then you can evaluate the pros and cons as a family at the end of the month.

Brainstorm several money-saving ideas you'd be willing to try for one month:

....

....

....

....

....

....

....

....

Barter: Would you prefer cooking while your friend prefers cleaning? Maybe you can swap services and you can provide her with some frozen meals in exchange for a couple hours of cleaning. Or maybe your "do-it-yourself" friends would have fun tackling a home improvement project as a couple in exchange for you taking their kids off their hands for the whole weekend. Bartering offers a great way to "pay" for help without spending a dime.

Make a list of your "bartering chips"—skills you have or tasks you find enjoyable:

....

....

....

....

....

....

....

....

....

....

Sell things: My mom always said that cash from doing things like having a garage sales or recycling soda cans was "found money." The practice of earning money from things you already have is a smart one! Think about ways you could earn some extra money to pay for hiring help. Maybe you could have a garage sale, sell books to a used bookstore, sell scrap metal, or sell old kids' clothes on Craigslist or on a Facebook buy/sell/trade group for your area. If you don't love it or haven't used it in a year, sell it! You will be amazed by how easily the money will add up.

Make a list of ten things you could sell to earn extra money.

....

....

....

....

....

....

....

....

....

....

I Will Embrace Help

One or more tasks I would like help with:

....

....

....

What steps will I need to take to get this help? (For example, talking with friends about swapping services, asking on Facebook for recommendations for cleaning or handyman services, or searching for options online.)

....

....

....

....

One concrete action I will take *this week* to show that I am embracing help:

....

....

....

....

Finish this sentence: *Embracing help will enable me to have a more creative and fulfilled life by . . .*

....

....

....

....

Fringe Principle 8

||||||||||||

I believe that
community matters.

Self-care doesn't only happen in isolation. Yes, solitude is an important element on the path toward a happier, more fulfilled you. However, one is never fully complete doing life as a loner. Only by sharing the path toward living well with a trusted community can you become the well-rounded woman God has created you to be.

All women need the encouragement and support of others along the way. In fact, some of my fondest memories involve being with people I love who inspire, challenge, and energize me. That's the kind of time spent that leaves me feeling filled up and better prepared to engage the next moment.

In my survey, 59 percent of the respondents reported that they sometimes enjoy doing what they love with another person. Let's face it—women like to be with other women. So it makes sense that when we're spending time doing something we love, we're often doing that something with *someone* we love.

Spending some of your fringe hours with others can lead to rich and fulfilling life experiences because you are meeting two needs at once—the need to do what you love and the need for relationships.

So consider practicing hobbies with others and asking for support when you need it.

Don't take your need for connection lightly. Pursue friendship and community wholeheartedly. The richness and love found in a bond that you share with another person (or persons) can bring to life something beautiful and meaningful inside of you.

"I have learned that to have a *good friend* is the *purest* of all God's gifts, for it is a *love* that has *no exchange* of payment."

FRANCES FARMER

Finding Your Fit

The beautiful thing about community is that it can happen in a variety of meaningful ways. Some women find happiness while connecting in a small quilting club. Others enjoy taking a jog with a friend. Still others love attending conferences with a large group. Sometimes the most fulfilling time happens over lunch or coffee with a best friend. Regardless of how it happens, the pursuit of living well is always made better when it's shared with people we love and who love us.

What kind of community do you enjoy most? One-on-one relationships? Small groups? Events?

one-on-one

small groups

events

What do you like about this kind of community?

....

....

....

....

What kind of things do you like to do in community? Circle any of the following ideas that you already enjoy doing with others or ones you might like to try:

Quilting	Concerts	Hiking
Scrapbooking	Bible study	Playing music
Exercise class	Spa outings	Painting/art
Book club	Cooking class	Dance
Cake decorating	Movies	Other: ....
Sewing/knitting	Crafting	

Describe the perfect afternoon spent with others:

....

....

....

....

....

....

....

....

....

....

For some, living in community isn't as easy as it sounds. Maybe that's you—perhaps you crave a community of people with whom to spend your fringe hours, but you aren't sure where to find it. Here are some helpful resources to get you started:

1. **Ask a friend:** This might seem like the most obvious, but ask others if they know of a particular resource you are searching for. You might be surprised what they recommend.

2. **Web search:** Type in your interest + your city and see what groups or clubs you find.

3. **Meetup.com:** This site strives to connect people who want to learn, do, or share something together.

4. **Church:** Some churches offer women's groups centered around different hobbies.

5. **Gym:** Gyms often offer a plethora of classes and interest groups. Check out ClassPass if you want to try different teaching environments.

6. **Area universities:** If you live in a university town, it may offer classes and meetups around certain interests.

7. **Community center:** Local community education programs often offer a wide range of enrichment opportunities ranging from computer basics to languages.

8. **Online:** A multitude of message boards and classes can be found on the internet. If you can't find anything that meets in person, an online forum or Facebook group is a good place to start.

Friends

Pursuing community around your hobbies and interests often results in friendships. Sometimes you meet a friend first and your similar personalities naturally lead you to spending free time with each other. Other times, the friendship is birthed from time spent together over a shared passion. But however they transpire, supportive friendships are a beautiful thing to build and nourish during your fringe hours.

What are the top three qualities that you look for in a friend?

....

....

....

....

Look at the list you just made. Do you see those qualities in yourself? Circle any of the qualities that you'd like to work on cultivating in your own heart. Having great friends starts with *being* a great friend.

"Let us be *grateful* to people who make us happy. They are the *charming gardeners* who make our *souls blossom*."

MARCEL PROUST

Who have been some of your best friends over the years? If any of these friends are no longer close, would you like to rekindle any of those relationships?

....

....

....

....

Have any of your relationships become unhealthy? If so, how can you protect your fringe hours from people who are pulling you down or draining your energy?

....

....

....

....

Have you ever been hurt by a friend? What did you learn from this experience and how can the lessons serve you today?

....

....

....

....

"One of the most
beautiful qualities of
true friendship
is to
understand and
to be understood."

LUCIUS ANNAEUS SENECA

Who's Your Encourager?

We all need someone in our lives who encourages us to pursue our passions and to take care of ourselves. It might be a spouse, sibling, co-worker, or friend. But without someone to cheer us on in our quest for self-care, we can easily fall into the traps of guilt and unrealistic expectations.

Who encourages you to invest in self-care?

....

....

....

How quick are you to let that person know when you need time for yourself?

....

....

....

Maybe the idea of someone telling you to "take care of yourself" makes you feel like laughing—or crying. You might not have *any* cheerleaders right now. But you can ask someone to be that person for you. We all need someone to help us and hold us accountable to self-care. Potential encouragers might include family members, co-workers, friends, church members, neighbors, or your spouse.

List two people you could ask to be your personal cheerleader:

....

....

Blending It All Together

Sometimes community, passions, and real-life responsibilities collide in a lovely, almost divine way. For instance, maybe you enjoy a night of cooking with girlfriends and come home with a week's worth of meals to put in the freezer. Or perhaps you finally take a small group jewelry-making class you've always thought about, and you end up creating a perfect birthday gift for your mom. Whatever your passion, learning a new skill during your fringe hours can lead to a practical payoff in your everyday world!

Have you ever thought, "It'd be fun to learn how to do that"? Make a list of hobbies or skills that you'd be interested in learning. Then put a star next to the ones you could do with a friend.

....

....

....

....

....

....

....

Look at the list you just made. For each item, brainstorm and write down one way you could use that skill to handle real-life responsibilities.

....

....

....

....

....

....

....

....

....

....

....

....

....

I Will Make Community Matter

Where am I already engaged in community and friendships? Do I feel good about the amount of time I invest in these people? Am I intentionally cultivating these relationships?

....

....

....

....

What personal passions or interests would I like to pursue with other people?

....

....

....

....

One concrete step I can take *this week* to show that community matters to me:

....

....

....

Finish this sentence: *Prioritizing community will enable me to have a more creative and fulfilled life by . . .*

....

....

....

....

Fringe Principle 9

||||||||||||

I believe in giving thanks and choosing joy.

Even when the days are packed full and feel as though they might never end, it is possible to intentionally choose gratitude and joy rather than stress and worry. In discovering your fringe hours and filling those segments of time with something that you love, you will find more reasons to be thankful. Choosing joy and embracing gratitude will feel more natural because you have given yourself the gift of time to *be* more of the person you desire to be.

Making time for you isn't just about what you do during that time; it's also about the ripple effect that it has on the rest of your days, your weeks, your life. Life's joys can be intensified when we invest in ourselves. By nurturing the gifts that we have or pursuing the quiet that our bodies crave, we're able to come away refreshed and ready for the challenges ahead.

Choose gratitude. Choose joy. Choose to be the woman you were created to be.

Giving Thanks

Gratitude transforms us from the inside out. A grateful heart is more joyful, more patient, and more full of grace. With a grateful outlook, you become present and able to savor the big and little gifts in your days.

Take time to consider the gifts in your life.

People I am grateful for:

....

....

....

....

Experiences I am grateful for:

....

....

....

....

Things I am grateful for:

....

....

....

....

For one week, write down three things you are thankful for every day.

Day 1: ....
....
....

Day 2: ....
....
....

Day 3: ....
....
....

Day 4: ....
....
....

Day 5: ....
....
....

Day 6: ....
....
....

Day 7: ....
....
....

Simple Ways to Say Thanks

Often we put off expressing our appreciation for others because we think it has to be a grand gesture. It doesn't! Here are a few simple ideas you can fit into your fringe hours:

If you have one minute: send someone a text.

If you have five minutes: write a card.

If you have ten minutes: give them a call.

If you have an hour: take them out for coffee on you.

"The practice of *gratitude* can *increase happiness* levels by around 25 percent."

DR. ROBERT EMMONS

"Whoever is
happy
will make others
happy too."

ANNE FRANK

Full of Joy

Have you ever noticed that some people just go through life with an attitude of joy? They tend to have a smile on their face, even when life's not always going their way. They notice the silver linings in even the darkest clouds.

My friend Sara was like that. Even though she was homebound and lived with a debilitating disease, she always chose joy. She reminded me that even in the darkest days, we can live well. Our circumstances do not have to control our spirit.

Think of someone in your life who emanates joy. What is it about that person that draws you to them?

....

....

....

....

Have you ever told this person that they have impacted you? If not, write down a way you will tell them how they have impacted your life (card, phone call, dinner date, etc.).

....

....

....

....

Joy to Your World

Joy is manifested in many ways—from a loved one to a sunset. Encountering joy creates a positive spark deep in our souls. Even amid challenges or obstacles, joy can show up and lighten the weight on our hearts.

What brings *you* joy? Make a list of the people, places, or things that cause joy in your life.

....

....

....

Make a list of things to love and celebrate about *you*.

My personality strengths:

....

....

My lovable quirks:

....

....

My talents/interests:

....

....

My roles/relationships:

....

....

I Will Live a Life of Thanksgiving and Joy

Where do I already consistently experience joy?

....

....

....

How did practicing gratitude every day for a week change my outlook?

....

....

....

....

One concrete step I can take *this week* to live in a place of thanksgiving and joy:

....

....

....

....

Finish this sentence: *Living with joy and thanksgiving will help me have a more creative and fulfilled life by . . .*

....

....

....

....

Final Reflections:
A Beautiful Life

*Y*ou've covered much ground in this book—recognizing the importance of self-care, searching your schedule for those precious moments you can seize for yourself, exploring passions and interests that you may have neglected or forgotten for years. My hope is that this process has inspired you to see the profound beauty and benefits that happen when you intentionally begin investing more fully in you—those experiences you encounter, those passions you rediscover, the community that joins you, and the fulfillment you feel when you look in the mirror and see a happier, more well-rounded, more complete you.

But trust me, after hearing from thousands of women across the country, I realize that finding fringe hours isn't always easy. And the reasons why it's not easy vary depending on who we are and the complexities of our lives. For the majority of us, finding our fringe hours and using them faithfully will take time. It's a process. And during that process, we'll have days and weeks when we find every reason or excuse to forego our need to take care of ourselves.

But don't beat yourself up. Instead, embrace the messiness of the process. Don't allow life's complicated and busy elements to prevent you from continuously working toward carving out moments for you. Over time, your life will become richer and more fulfilled as practicing self-care becomes habitual.

My prayer is that as you make time for yourself, you will grow more confident in who you are and experience deeper satisfaction with how you spend your time. I believe that as you pursue the practice of self-care, your life will become defined by gratitude and joy—not because you've done it all perfectly but because you've realized what God knew all along: that *you* are a unique and one-of-a-kind treasure. And this world needs you—the best possible you.

So go ahead. Sign up for that knitting class. Take a long run. Pull out that journal and start filling its blank pages. Make yourself a priority. Invest time in the you that God made you to be. Because you are worth it.

This is your new beginning—and it's going to be beautiful.

"The longer
I live, the more
beautiful
life becomes."

FRANK LLOYD WRIGHT

⫸⟶

What is your definition of beauty?

....
....
....
....
....
....
....
....
....

beauty: 1. a combination of qualities,
such as shape, color, or form,
that pleases the aesthetic senses,
especially the sight. 2. a beautiful or
pleasing thing or person, in particular

List ten beautiful things in your life right now.

1. ....

2. ....

3. ....

4. ....

5. ....

6. ....

7. ....

8. ....

9. ....

10. ....

Tape a picture here of something
beautiful in your life.

My Fringe Hours Commitment

Starting today, I will make my life more beautiful by living according to these principles:

I believe in cultivating balance in my commitments and within myself.

I believe in letting go of self-imposed pressures.

I believe that guilt and comparison do not belong in my life.

I believe that I can make time for myself.

I believe that pursuing my passions is life-giving and life changing.

I believe that taking care of my mind, body, and soul is important.

I believe in embracing help.

I believe that community matters.

I believe in giving thanks and choosing joy.

Signature: .... Date: ....

"Life is not perfect. **You** are not perfect. But you are a *glorious creation*, and your life is meant to be lived with *joy."*

Survey Data

1. How much time do you spend weekly on yourself and the things you are passionate about?

a.	less than an hour	3%
b.	1-3 hours	36%
c.	3-5 hours	25%
d.	5-9 hours	20%
e.	10-14 hours	10%
f.	15 hours or more	6%

2. What kinds of activities do you love to do?

a.	Outdoor activities	41%
b.	Exercising	43%
c.	Sewing/knitting/crocheting	27%
d.	Playing an instrument	10%
e.	Crafting	41%
f.	Spa time	26%
g.	Reading	86%
h.	Collecting	4%
i.	Scrapbooking	27%
j.	Photography	33%
k.	Cooking/baking	50%

l.	Writing	24%
m.	Blogging	23%
n.	Other	20%

3. Do you ever do these activities with other people?

a.	Yes, with one other person	42%
b.	Yes, with a small group of people	43%
c.	Yes, with a large group of people	6%
d.	No	41%

4. On a scale from 0 to 10, how satisfied are you with the amount of time you have for yourself?

0	5%
1	6%
2	12%
3	14%
4	11%
5	13%
6	9%
7	11%
8	8%
9	5%
10	6%

5. If you had more time, what activities would you do or do more of?

a.	Outdoor activities	37%
b.	Exercising	54%
c.	Sewing/knitting/crocheting	26%
d.	Playing an instrument	14%
e.	Crafting	35%
f.	Spa time	27%
g.	Reading	59%
h.	Collecting	3%
i.	Scrapbooking	28%
j.	Photography	30%
k.	Cooking/baking	38%
l.	Writing	28%
m.	Blogging	21%
n.	Other	12%

6. During the week, what time do you wake up?

a.	Before 5 a.m.	5%
b.	5:00 to 5:59 a.m.	29%
c.	6:00 to 6:59 a.m.	41%
d.	7:00 to 7:59 a.m.	18%
e.	8:00 a.m. or later	7%

7. If you have children, do you wake up before, at the same time as, or after your children?

a.	Before my children	61%
b.	At the same time as my children	36%
c.	After my children	3%

8. On average, how many nights a week are you not at home due to other commitments?

1	37%
2	26%
3	19%
4	11%
5	4%
6	2%
7	<1%

9. What time do you go to bed?

a.	Before 9 p.m.	2%
b.	9:00 to 9:59 p.m.	17%
c.	10:00 to 10:59 p.m.	41%
d.	11:00 to 11:59 p.m.	29%
e.	12 a.m. or later	11%

10. If you have children, do you go to bed before, at the same time as, or after your children?

a.	Before my children	3%
b.	At the same time as my children	8%
c.	After my children	88%

11. When do you find time to do the things that you love?

a.	In the morning	35%
b.	At lunch time	13%
c.	In the afternoon	27%
d.	At dinnertime	4%
e.	In the evening	75%
f.	During other activities	26%

12. What are the barriers to making time for yourself?

a.	Work	58%
b.	Kids	59%
c.	Household responsibilities	79%
d.	Spouse/significant other	35%
e.	Finances	41%
f.	Church	14%
g.	Group activities	6%
h.	Other	14%

13. Does someone in your life encourage you to make time for yourself?

Yes	68%
No	32%

If so, who?

a.	Spouse/significant other	80%
b.	Relative	29%
c.	Friend	41%

14. Do you have the following devices/technology in your home?

a.	Smartphone	82%
b.	iPad/tablet	61%
c.	E-reader	43%
d.	Cable or satellite TV	67%
e.	Laptop or desktop computer	97%
f.	Internet	96%

15. Do you pay for any of the following services?

a.	Child care	20%
b.	Cleaning service	12%
c.	Lawn service	13%
d.	Laundry service	2%
e.	Meal preparation	1%
f.	Handyman service	6%

16. Do you keep a calendar?

Yes	96%
No	4%

If yes, what type of calendar do you use?

a.	Wall calendar	45%
b.	Portable paper planner	40%
c.	Calendar on phone	55%
d.	Calendar on computer	39%

17. Do you use any productivity apps? Most frequently cited apps were Evernote, Apple's Notes and Reminders, Cozi, and Wunderlist.

In addition to the information reflected in the preceding pages, women who participated in the Fringe Hours Survey provided nearly five hundred pages of commentary in response to the following questions:

18. If you make time for yourself, why do you value doing that?

19. If you don't make time for yourself, why don't you?

20. What do you think is most challenging about being a woman today?

Jessica N. Turner is the founder of the popular lifestyle blog *The Mom Creative*, where she documents her pursuit of cultivating a life well crafted (TheMomCreative.com). She is a writer for HuffPost Parents, Parenting.com, and DaySpring's (in)courage. She is also an advocate for World Vision, a regular speaker at conferences nationwide, and an award-winning marketing professional. She and her husband, Matthew, live with their three young children in Nashville, Tennessee.

For inspiring content about motherhood,
DIY projects, frugal living, product reviews,
and more, visit Jessica's lifestyle blog,

TheMomCreative.com

Also connect with her via social media:

- Facebook.com/TheMomCreative
- Twitter.com/JessicaNTurner
- Pinterest.com/JessicaNTurner
- Instagram.com/JessicaNTurner
- YouTube.com/TheMomCreative

Useful Resources for You

Visit **FringeHours.com** for information and resources to help you
on your journey toward making time for you.

You'll find:

- Free downloads

- Useful videos

- Product recommendations

- Book club resources

- And more!

Also check out #FringeHours on Instagram and Twitter
for inspiration from other women using their fringe hours.

Have You Read the Book

that changed how women find time for themselves?

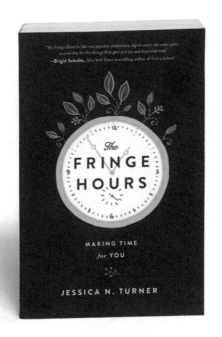

" *The Fringe Hours* is like one gigantic permission slip to carve out some space in your day for the things that give you joy and feed your soul."
—Brigid Schulte. *New York Times* bestselling author of *Overwhelmed*

THE FRINGE HOURS PRODUCTS

Practical and inspiring products developed with Jessica for you. Including a variety of cards, notebooks and organizers, this collection will encourage you to use your fringe hours well.

You can find these at dayspring.com/fringehours

Follow us on twitter @incourage